WESTERN EDUCATION AND LIBRARY BOARD.
LIBRARY SERVICE.

GLOUCESTER HOUSE

Books can be renewed, by personal application, post or telephone, quoting latest date, author and book number.

NO RENEWALS CAN BE GRANTED FOR A BOOK RESERVED BY ANOTHER READER.

Readers are expected to take care of books. Lost or damaged books must be paid for by the borrower concerned.
PD 58

How to

Make masks

Michael Kingsley Skinner

Studio Vista London

Acknowledgments

Photographs are by Kenneth Broome of Humphrey Stevens, Ewell, Surrey. The author would also like to thank Timothy Dolby, Elizabeth, Mark and Sarah, together with many of the pupils of Rydens School, for all their help and co-operation.

Text and drawings copyright © 1973 by Michael Skinner
Photographs copyright © 1973 by Studio Vista

Published in Great Britain by
Studio Vista
Blue Star House, Highgate Hill, London N19

Filmset, printed and bound in England by
BAS Printers Limited, Wallop, Hampshire

ISBN 0 289 70337 9

Contents

Introduction

This book was written to show what fun can be had from the making and designing of a wide variety of masks. At the same time it gives opportunities for experimenting with different materials and for using one's design sense to the full.

Most people like to create something and I feel this will give them not only the chance to make useful masks for parties and plays but also a great deal of pleasure and satisfaction.

Masks have been made for thousands of years and for a variety of reasons—for fun and amusement, for unpleasant occasions, in order to terrify at ceremonies, for parties or carnivals, and for the stage. All of them were made to disguise.

Try making faces in the mirror and see what a variety of changes you can make to your appearance by looking happy, sad and so on—try!

M.K.S.

Warning!

It can be dangerous to cover your face completely with a mask. Do make sure before you put on any mask that you will be able to breathe properly when it is in position.

Simple folded masks

You need: a rectangular piece of stiff card or paper
cutting knife and string

Fold the paper or card in half. Hold it in front of
your face with the fold in the centre, and mark on
it with a pencil the position of your eyes. Now
remove the paper from your face and cut holes for
eyes with a sharp knife. They could be circles,
triangles or squares. Cut away the bottom left-hand
corner of the folded mask, **a**, to leave your nose and
mouth free.

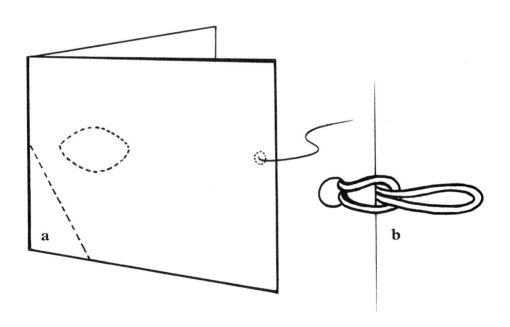

The sides can be shaped to look like a highwayman's mask. Make holes at the sides with a sharp point (a pencil will do) so that you can thread string through. First strengthen the holes with extra card or adhesive tape, as the strain on the mask is likely to tear the card before it has had much use. You can now tie the strings at the back of your head. As an alternative, elastic bands can be looped through the holes (diagram **b**, page 7) and then stretched over your ears.

On the facing page are more designs for folded masks.

Folded mask with further decoration

Fold the stiff paper or card down the centre as
before, but to make the mask more decorative cut
the outer edge of the folded card into more interesting shapes. Simple and bold treatment is usually
the most effective as the more detailed cuts will not
be seen from a distance.

Draw your design onto the card first if you wish.
It will help you plan more carefully the effect you
want.

When the shape is finished you can make it look even more effective by decorating the surface with bold patterns and designs.

To add to the decoration the stiff paper or card can easily be made to curl by cutting strips (see facing page) and rolling them round a pencil. This treatment is useful for hair, beards, and so on.

See pages 62 and 63 for further ideas for decoration.

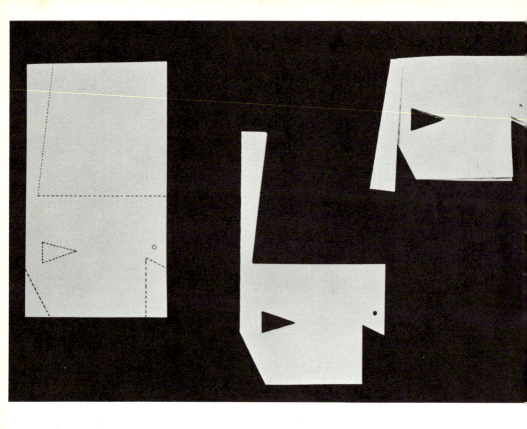

Folded mask with nose and ears

Fold the card or paper in the usual way but add
an extra vertical shape at the top of your original
folded mask for the nose as shown opposite. Cut
out eye shapes and a space for the nose as before.
When the vertical shape is bent down over the
mask it will stick out in front.

Remember that the mask is cut double. The fold
runs down the left-hand side of the diagrams.
When the nose is bent down, the fold down the
middle of the nose will have to be reversed. You may
need to add an adhesive hinge behind the nose to
prevent it flapping.

Cut the ear shapes from the sides of the existing mask and bend them forward. Remember that both nose and ear shapes can vary according to the character you are making.

You can add eyebrows or moustaches in the same way as the nose. Simply cut an extra piece at the top of the mask and fold it down. On page 14 are sketches of the kinds of masks you might make.

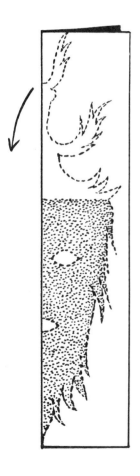

14

Mask with pointed nose

To make a very pointed nose for your mask you
will have to add another piece of folded card,
as shown in the diagram. Fix it to the top of
the corner you cut away for the nose and mouth.
Fold a triangular piece of card, **a**, down the middle
or use the V-shaped corner you have cut away from
the mask. Cut a small V-shape in it, **b**. Fold along
both sides of the V, diagram **c**, to make flaps.
You can now glue the flaps to the back of the mask.

Instead of a pointed nose you could make a bird's beak for your mask. Follow the instructions on page 15. One of these was decorated with macaroni and other kinds of pasta, the other was covered with feathers.

The colourful cone-shapes and tube masks shown opposite are very easy indeed to make. See pages 22 and 24 for instructions.

16

Above: a folded mask as described on page 10 makes a very effective king.

Left: the fiery dragon (see page 43) was made from plaster of Paris bandages on a wire frame

19

Adjustable masks

Basic shape

You need: thin card or stiff paper
craft knife, split staple

This will be worn like a helmet or a hat. Fold the
card as before but lengthen the 'nose shape' so that
it will stretch right back over the head. Cut long
pieces at the sides to go round your head and meet
at the back.

The three strips of card are pinned together by
split staples at the back so that the size can be
altered according to the wearer.

When fitting the mask make sure that the strips are
comfortable and that the wearer can move freely.

You can add to this basic shape in all kinds of ways.
Give it a large nose or beak as described on page 15,
or add a headdress like those in the sketches opposite.

21

Cone-shaped mask

(colour photograph page 17)

You need: card
cutting knife
adhesive tape

Cut a piece of card about 45 cm. (or 18 in.) wide according to the size of your head. Bend it into a cone shape. Place it onto a cone shape. Place it over your head and mark the position of your eyes and mouth. Lay the card flat again and cut out the features. Bend it into the cone shape again and fix it with adhesive tape. Additional features and decorations can now be added — eyebrows, moustache, nose, hair, etc.

It is easy to turn the top of the cone mask into a hat. A witch's hat can be made by dropping a circle of card, with a hole cut in the centre, over the point of the cone. Start by cutting a small hole and then make it gradually larger until the brim comes down to the right position on the cone.

Masks from cardboard tubes

(colour photograph page 17)

You need: card, cutting knife, adhesive tape

Cut a rectangular piece of card, large enough to
fit round your head and rest on your shoulders.

Measure and mark the centre of the card. This
will be a guide in marking out the position of the
eyes, nose and mouth. Cut these out of the card with
a sharp knife.

Bend the card carefully into a tube, overlapping
the ends by at least 2·5 cm. (or 1 in.). Fix with
staples or strong adhesive tape.

You can now draw in or cut out additional features
such as a nose, eyebrows, horns, a crown, a hat,
etc. Make sure these are fixed firmly before painting
and decorating.

Experiment with very short, wide tubes or very long
tubes, or tubes that taper slightly and are wide
enough at the bottom to rest on your shoulders.

Buckram mask

You need: clay, plasticine, or a similar modelling
material
modelling board
buckram
string

You will need to make a mould for your buckram
mask by modelling the face in clay or plasticine.
Measure the outline of your face with a piece of
string. Lay the string on the board and mark the
outline onto it.

Now model the face within the outline, gradually
building up the features.

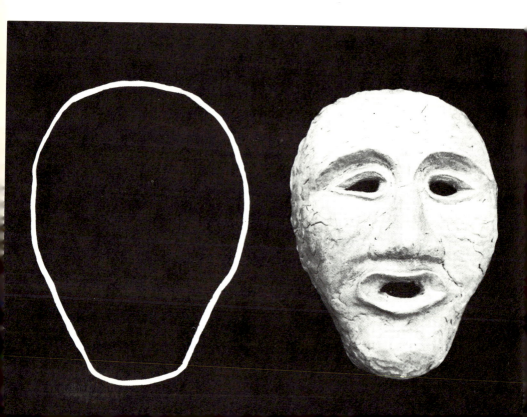

Buckram is a stiff material used in the making of hats. It can be bought in most large drapers' stores. Half a yard is sufficient for two masks. The advantage of this material is that when dipped in water and squeezed gently it becomes soft and on drying it regains its stiffness.

Lay the damp soft buckram over the finished clay model and press it carefully onto the face. A small stick or pencil is useful for this.

Leave it to dry thoroughly before removing the buckram from the mould and trimming round the edge.

When you paint the mask, use as little water with the paint as possible, or the buckram will begin to lose its shape. Felt-tipped pens are good for decorating this kind of material.

To make the mask extra strong, cover the buckram with a couple of layers of paper and paste before decorating it.

These are both buckram masks, one painted with a clown's face and the other with an equally effective abstract design. The clown has a paper frill round his neck to make him look even more authentic.

Now that you have made one buckram mask, experiment with different facial expressions. Make some faces in the mirror. You will see that when you look happy, sad, worried or petrified, it is mainly the shape of your eyes and mouth that change.

Now try modelling faces with different eye and mouth shapes and use the best ones for making buckram masks.

Square masks

You need: *either* a cardboard box *or* a sheet of
thin cardboard about 36 cm. (or 14 in.)
long and 25 cm. (or 10 in.) wide
scissors
glue
sticky tape
paint

base
either: Cut away two opposite sides of the box
or: Make a fold 7·5 cm (or 3 in.) in from each end
of the sheet of cardboard. Strengthen the edges
and sides with sticky tape. Coloured tape could be
used as a decoration.

Cut out holes for the eyes, nose and mouth.

nose
Glue on a small box or a piece of folded cardboard.

eyes
Sections cut from plastic egg boxes make good
'robot's' eyes. Cut a hole in the end of each section
before gluing it in position so that you will be able to
see out clearly.

Paint or spray the mask.

31

Papier-mâché mask

You need: clay or
             plasticine
           Vaseline
           tissue paper
           newspaper
           cold water
             cellulose
             paste (or
             flour paste)
           brush
           modelling board

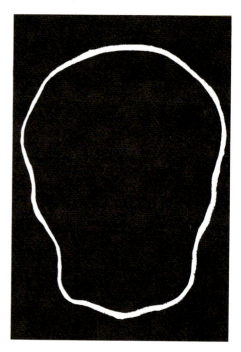

First a clay or plasticine
mould has to be made.
Draw onto the board an
outline of the face to be
modelled. Now start to
model within the outline
building up the features
in clay or plasticine. Make
them bold and generous;
avoid fiddly detail.

If you are using
plasticine and it is hard,
it can be softened by
immersing it for a while
in warm water. Dry it in
a towel and then knead it
with both hands.

When you are satisfied
with the modelling a start
can be made on the mask.

32

Grease the mould well with Vaseline. This will allow the finished mask to be removed easily, without spoiling the modelling. You will then be able to use the mould again and again.

Cut up some tissue paper into squares of about 4 cm. (or 1·5 in.) to cover the mould, overlapping each square. The paper will stick to the Vaseline.

When the mould is completely covered start applying newspaper squares which have been soaked in water, overlapping each square and pasting layer after layer. Five layers will be sufficiently strong. Use your fingers and paste brush to press the paper into the various shapes on the mould.

Allow the mask to dry thoroughly before attempting to remove it from the mould. When it is dry carefully lift the mask from the mould. Any small tears can be made good with paste and paper later.

You are now ready to paint and decorate the mask. Emulsion paints are good for this. Seeds, string, etc. can add to the decoration.

Fix a piece of elastic or string at the sides of the mask at eye level.

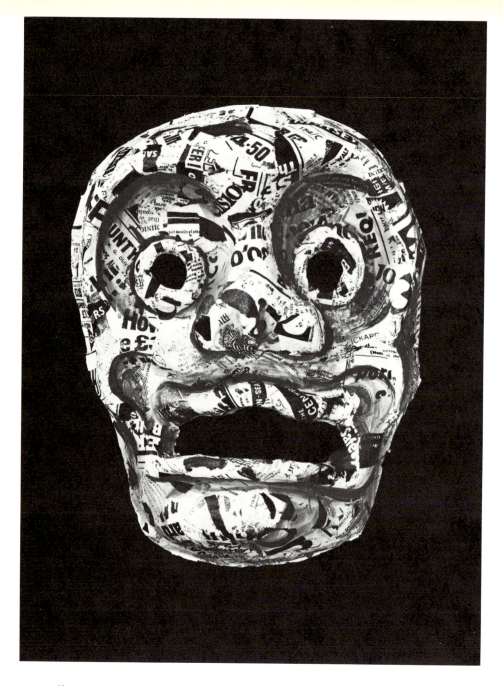

Above and opposite:
A papier-mâché mask before and after decoration

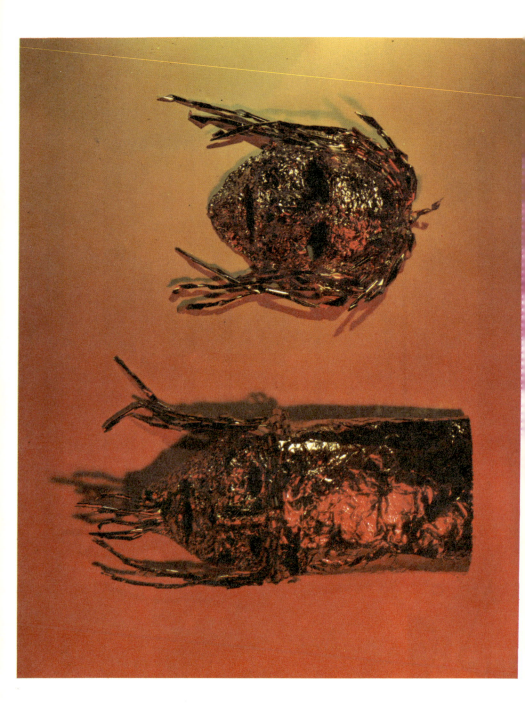

Tinfoil portrait mask

You need: tinfoil (the kind used for cooking)
           fibreglass resin (see page 66)
           brush

This kind of mask is difficult to make on yourself
so a friend will be needed to act as a model.

Cut a piece of tinfoil large enough to cover the
face. Place the foil over the face and ask the model
to hold it at the top of his head. This leaves both
your hands free to 'feel' and carefully press the foil
over and around the shape of the face, including the
bone structure of the chin.

Only when the whole face has been carefully worked
can the mask be removed. But make sure you do not
take too long!

The mask will now have to be strengthened from
the inside with several coats of fibreglass resin.
See page 66 for details of materials. Cut out the
eyes and nostrils and add further details such as a
headress, etc. if you wish.

Coloured sticky tape and self-adhesive shapes can
be used very effectively for decorating this type of
mask and strips of tinfoil can be curled to make
hair and beards as on the facing page.

Other ways of using foil

Neo-Fol, which can be purchased at art shops, is a
thicker material and unsuitable for portrait masks,
but when used for decoration or for simple
folded masks (see pages 7–13) it can produce very
effective and exciting results. Detailed decoration
can be applied by pressing a pencil into the Neo-Fol
while it is on a soft surface.

To strengthen the mask you will need to paint
coats of fibreglass resin onto the reverse side,
or you could glue it to some sheeting, book muslin,
or similar material.

Useful pieces of foil can be salvaged from pie and
pastry cases and can be used in the same way as
above or for smaller decoration.

Interesting effects can be achieved when ordinary
sheet cooking foil is glued over objects already fixed to
a mask. You can cover things like string, twigs,
seeds, curtain rings, matches, and so on. Emulsion
paint is good for painting in the background.

The mask opposite was made from card, with the
features marked out in plasticine, and covered with
foil. The background was painted with black
emulsion.

Big carnival heads

You need: narrow gauge wire mesh (the kind used in the making of chicken runs), wire cutters, old newspapers, two pints of cellulose paste, brush and paints.

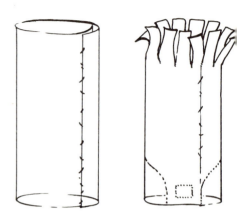

Bend the mesh into a tube. The size will of course vary according to your needs, but the one illustrated on page 42 measures about 1·5 m. round by 95 cm. tall.

Make a series of cuts about 20 cm. (or 8 in.) deep round the top of the tube. These must be bent inwards to form a dome. Add separate pieces of wire for the nose, mouth and eyebrows. Squeeze or pleat the wire at the bottom to form the neck.

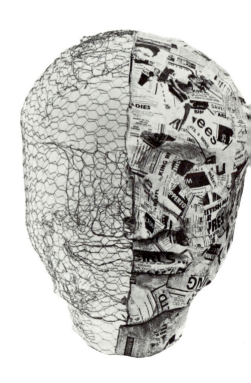

The wire structure must now be covered with 2–3 layers of pasted paper using pieces about 10 cm. (4 in.) square and overlapping each piece. These few layers will be sufficient

as the strength of the head is in the wire structure. The paste must soak the paper thoroughly before it is applied. This job can be messy and as the head is large it is best to do this in the yard or garden.

Allow the head to dry thoroughly before painting. Use one coat of a household emulsion type paint. This will give a good base for your decoration and prevent the printing on the pasted paper showing through. If water colour paints are used in the final decoration a coat of varnish should be applied all over the head to protect it and make it waterproof.

Take great care with the finish on the inside of the neck, which fits over the head of the wearer. Make absolutely sure that no wire is left sticking out that will scratch the face. Foam rubber or material could be glued inside.

The next job is to make an eye hole in the neck to enable the wearer to see comfortably. Mark it and cut it out with wire cutters, binding the edges with sticky tape.

Stitch four long tapes to the front and back of the neck, so that the head can be tied round the waist to keep the head in position. You can give added ventilation by making holes in ears, nostrils and mouth of the head or by incorporating them in part of the pattern or design.

Of course you can add 'extras' in the form of hats, spectacles, collar and tie, and hair of hemp or wire wool.

Wire frame masks

You need: Wire which can easily bend
and is pliable enough to allow
pieces to be twisted together
to make joins. If a large model
is to be made, the same
wire can be used double by
twisting two pieces together
for extra strength.
A roll of brown sticky
paper as used in packag-
ing. Scissors, sponge, brush and
paints.

For more complicated shapes you will need to
make a wire frame. These can be made to fit your
face or to go right over your head like the 'Big heads'.

Draw the main outline of the head on paper, then
bend the wire round the outline. Start building up
the frame by making a series of wire loops which
will give roundness to the mask and at the same
time give support to the outline. These loops should
be about 6 cm. (or 2·5 in.) apart. Make sure the wire
is firm and try not to leave any sharp ends sticking
out.

Use a sponge to damp lengths of the sticky paper,
looping them over the wire and sticking the ends at
the back. Continue in this way till the frame is
completely covered.

You can now paint the mask or decorate it by covering
it completely with glue and sprinkling grass seed or
something similar all over to give it an interesting

texture like coarse hair. The stag on the facing page was decorated in this way. Fur, sand, feathers and so on could also be used.

Plaster of Paris bandages were used instead of sticky paper to make this dragon (colour photograph page 18).

Masks from balloons

You need: balloon, newspaper, paste, Vaseline, brush, and paints

Blow up the balloon and tie a knot at the neck or tie a string round the end. Cover the balloon with a thin layer of liquid soap or Vaseline. This will allow it to come away easily from the model later.

You can now start to cover the surface with pieces of paste-soaked newspaper, allowing them to overlap each other. This will give the strength to the structure. Leave the area around the knotted end clear.

Continue to cover the balloon, building up 4–5 layers of paper all over it. It is important to try to cover it evenly so as to avoid creating weak areas.

This clown's face was built up on a balloon and given a ping-pong ball for a nose and some hair of hemp.

Alternative layers of different kinds of paper could be used—perhaps one layer of newspaper and one of kitchen paper, and so on.

Tie a piece of string round the knot and hang the balloon up to dry. Do not put it near a fire or radiator.
Make sure the model is quite dry and firm before you burst or untie the balloon and remove it.
You are now ready to cut the shape in half to make two masks. Use a craft knife or sharp scissors.

Place one shape over your face and mark the position of eyes and mouth. You can now begin to paint. Thick poster colour paints or powder colour mixed with Marvin Medium, Gel, or simply flour and water paste are ideal.

For attaching the mask to the head, fix elastic, tape or string on each side of the mask at eye level.

Masks of all shapes and sizes can be cut from your balloon shape to fit over the crown of your head like a helmet (see facing page).

Additional materials and features can be added quite easily. You could use ping-ping balls for noses (see clown mask page 47). Puncture and flatten them slightly before gluing. Sew or glue on hemp for hair. Add hats, large beaks of cardboard (see page 50), or even feathers. These are just a few suggestions for making a really striking mask.

Paper bag masks

You need: a large paper bag, as used by refuse
           collectors
           scissors and paints

Mark and cut at the top of the bag (the sealed end)
the position of your eyes, nose and mouth. You
can do this by holding the bag in front of your face.

Cut two holes on the sides of the bag approximately
30 cm. (or 12 in.) from the top for armholes.

You are now ready to paint and decorate it. Both
sides of the bag can be decorated. Try painting
a different character on each side.

Other forms of decoration can be used as well
as painting—coloured papers, raffia, string, leaves,
seeds, feathers, and so on, simply by sticking them
onto the bag.

On the next two pages are all kinds of ideas for
decorating these 'masks'.

Opposite This unusual bird was made from a 'balloon mask' and the
large cardboard beak was glued in position afterwards.

52

Using string for masks

You need: thin card, string, glue, scissors.

Take a piece of card larger than the size of your
own face. This will allow for extra decoration.
Mark on the card the positions of your eyes, nose
and mouth and cut them out.

Lay the mask flat on some old newspaper and cover
it generously with glue. Now lay lengths of string on
the wet glue in various patterns. You could coil it
round the eyes and mouth, or you could plait it
first. Or you could unravel it to use it as hair, beards,
moustaches, etc. Try to cover all the card as this is
intended only as backing and not part of the design.

String could be coiled round a cardboard cone for
a nose. Experiment to find your own variations.
Remember that you would use different coloured
strings as part of the design.

Allow the glue to dry perfectly before moving the
mask. No further decoration is necessary, but if
certain areas of cardboard remain undecorated you
could add interesting textures, or you could paint or
spray them.

Glue, tie or sew string firmly at the sides at eye
level for attaching the mask to the head.

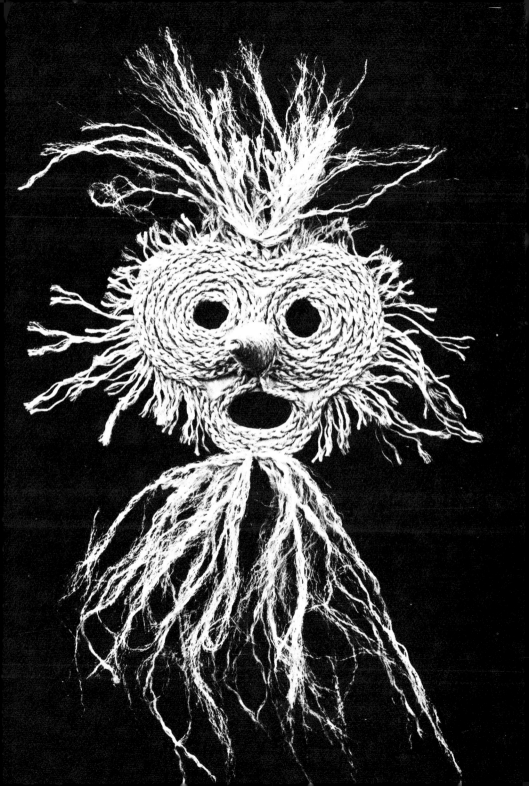

Corrugated cardboard masks

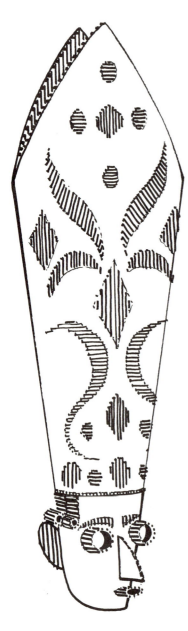

You need: corrugated
                cardboard
            size
            glue
            scissors

This material is ideal for
mask-making as it curves
around the face so well.
Very interesting effects
can be achieved by con-
trasting rough and smooth,
using different colours, or
by cutting and rolling.

A wash of size over the
surface will make the mask
stronger. You could cover
the inside of the mask with
glue and a layer of book
muslin or similar material.

Dishcloth masks

You need: a dishcloth, rag, or piece of loosely
              woven material
           starch
           bucket or large jar

Make up a strong solution of starch, using two good
tablespoons of starch to one pint of water. Soak
the dishcloth in it.

Remove the cloth from the liquid and lay it over
a curved surface such as a bucket or wide curved
jar. Drag the material into the shape of eyebrows,
nose and mouth, and shape the outline of the face.
Leave it to dry.

Cut out the eyes and mouth and attach strings at
eye-level for attaching the mask to the head.

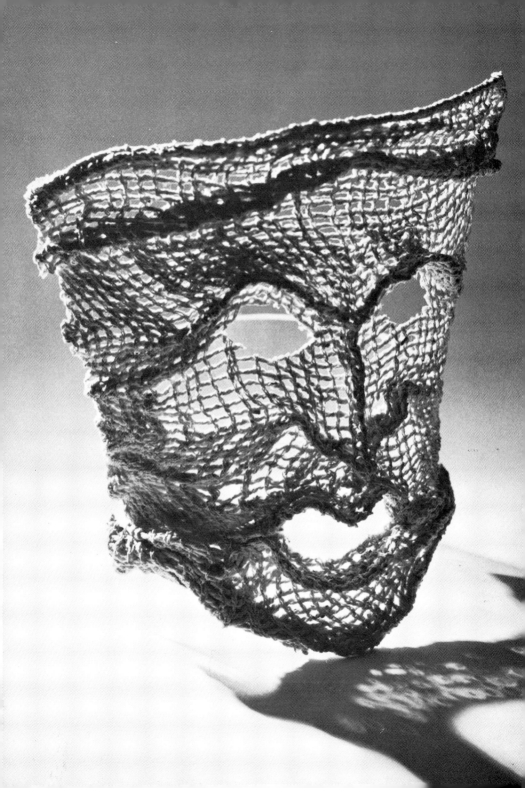

Polystyrene stick masks

You need: 1 or 2 polystyrene ceiling tiles
a glue suitable for use with polystyrene (some glues are not suitable as they eat into the material)
a small battery-operated cutter or a sharp knife which can also be used hot
paints
stick

Draw the outline of the mask on the tile and then cut it out. The mask should be large enough to cover the face well. Use the pieces you have cut away for the eyebrows, nose, mouth, etc. Stick these carefully in position and allow them to dry. The shapes could be built up one on top of the other to make the nose protrude. Each layer can be painted different colours.

Fix the stick firmly to the back of the mask with adhesive tape or glue it between two tiles and make a double-sided mask.

Thin polystyrene of the kind used for insulation is flexible and good to work with, but it cracks easily and should first be glued to fabric.

Stick masks need not be flat. Any of your curved masks could be attached to a stick.

Decoration and further suggestions

Wax crayons Cover the whole area of card with coloured waxes and draw patterns, lines, squares, circles, etc. Then completely cover the design with black wax. Now use a penknife to scrape through the black to reveal patches of the colours underneath.

Wax resist Draw a design in white wax on white card. Take a large soft brush and using ink or water colour paints, paint over the design lightly. At once you will see the design appearing. (page 8)

Coloured inks Inks are good on their own but interesting effects can be achieved when the paper or card is made wet and the inks are allowed to drop and run or be brushed over the surface. (page 11)

Collage The different treatments, materials and textures that this form of decoration can take must be endless, as the wide variety of natural and man-made materials available to us are enormous. Feathers, shells, seeds, peas, pips, felts, beads, old postage stamps, paper cut or torn from old magazines, string, paper clips, eggshells, sand, sugar, rice, woodshavings . . . all of these can be used with masks. Much fun can be derived from collecting these articles. After selecting the materials simply arrange them and glue them into position. (Example page 16)

Polyurethane foam This is very useful for filling the back of a Portrait Foil Mask or any mask that is to be used only for decoration. It dries quickly and can be cut and sawn very easily. Feathers etc. for headresses can be pushed into it. To make it you must mix the two liquids, using equal amounts by volume of each and stir well for twenty seconds.

Wallpaper Masks made from thick wallpapers can be interesting. Old pattern books are usually given away. See if your local paint and wallpaper store will let you have one.

Glasspapers Folded masks made from glasspapers give unusual textures.

Scraperboard This is a thin card covered with plaster and coated with black ink. It can be bought at most art and craft shops. The decoration is scraped through the black using a small pointed tool. Though these boards crack easily they can be strengthened with a backing.

Group Mask: Sea-serpent or caterpillar Big head masks can be extended with sheeting and wire loops to cover several wearers at once. Peepholes can be hidden in the pattern at various intervals.

Theatrical plastic modelling wax This is fun to use and easy to apply. Simply model it on to your own face exaggerating your ears, nose, etc. It may be bought from theatrical costumiers.

Old plastic buckets
These are light and can easily be converted into a complete mask. Cut out eyes, nose and mouth, adding a variety of decoration.

Masks used as decoration
Masks make splendid wall decoration, either mounted on different coloured backgrounds or placed straight on the wall. All you have to do is tie together the fixing strings at the back of the mask and hang it from a nail or hook on the wall. Lights behind or near the mask can give very interesting effects. Coloured lights shining on silver foil can be very dramatic (see page 38).

Materials and suppliers

Reeves and Sons Ltd., 13, Charing Cross Road, London, W.C.2.
All art materials including metal foil, paper and card, polymer colours and medium, plasticine, clay, varnish, coloured inks, silver and gold paint, coloured sellotape.

Charles H. Fox Ltd., (Theatrical Costumiers) 25, 25, Shelton Street, London, W.C.2.
Plastic modelling wax.

Prima Glassfibre Materials Ltd., Platt's Eyot, Lower Sunbury Road, Hampton-on-Thames, Middlesex.
Polyurethane Foam, fibreglass resin.

Polycell Products Ltd., Broadwater Road, Welwyn Garden City, Herts.
Polycell Paste.

T. J. Smith & Nephew, Hull.
Plaster of Paris bandages (Gypsona) (Can be purchased from most Chemists)

Trylon Ltd., Thrift Street, Wollaston, Northants. N.N.9 7QJ.
Polyurethane foam, fibreglass resin.

Marley Retail Ltd., Sevenoaks, Kent.
Cutta-mastic (polystyrene cutter)

Index